and the Birds

Written by Sarah Prince
Illustrated by Naomi C. Lewis

Once there was an old man named Benny.
Benny didn't have a dog, and he didn't
have a cat, but he had a hundred
birds! They were beautiful pigeons,
all different colors.

Benny loved them all very much, and he had a name for each one. Every morning, Benny was up bright and early. As soon as he opened the cages, the birds would fly high into the sky.

3

The birds would swoop and fly around and around in big circles above Benny's house.

Benny would smile as he watched his birds twisting and swooping and turning.
Then they would fly off for their day's adventure.

Later that day, Benny would wait for them to return.

One day Benny was not well.
He woke up in great pain and
could hardly walk.

The birds were still locked in their cages.
They knew that something was wrong.

Benny's friend, Edgar, came to visit
and found Benny sick in bed.
Edgar insisted that Benny go to the
hospital to see a doctor.

The doctor said, "Benny, you are getting old. Your heart is not strong. I would like to keep you here for a rest."

Suddenly Benny remembered his birds.

"Oh, my birds! What have I done!" he cried. "Edgar, please go quickly to my home. My birds are still locked in their cages. Please set them free."

8

Edgar hurried to Benny's house and opened every cage. The birds quickly flew out of the cages. Edgar waited for the birds to swoop and fly around and around in big circles above Benny's house. But instead, the birds flew straight up into the sky and out of sight.

Later that day, Edgar returned
to lock up the birds for the night.
He waited and waited, but the birds
did not return.

What would he tell his dear friend
Benny? The birds were all Benny had.

Edgar worried all of the way to
the hospital. He stood outside Benny's
room, afraid to tell him the awful news.

He opened the door, and what did he see?

Birds! Birds! They were everywhere—on the windowsill, on the chair, on the table, and all over the bed.

And right in the middle
was Benny's smiling face.

Benny's dearest friends had come
to make him well.

"My heart may not be strong, but it's
big enough to love all of my friends,"
said Benny.